ADVENTURE WITH PINEY JOE

Exploring the New Jersey Pine Barrens
Volumes I & II

Story by William J. Lewis
Illustrations by Shane Tomalinas

Adventure with

Adventure with Piney Joe: Exploring the New Jersey Pine Barrens, Volumes I & II.

Published by the South Jersey Culture & History Center Regional Press.

ISBN: 978-1-947889-09-5

Explore this Book!

Introduction   7

Adventure with Piney Joe, Volume I   11

"The Pine Gnome"   56

Adventure with Piney Joe, Volume II   61

Piney Joe's Self-Guided Exploration Trail Map   109

Where to Explore Next   172

Acknowledgements   174

Plant List   177

Plant Index   177

About the Author   180

About the Illustrator   181

Gucci Green Afterword   182

Adventure with

Dedication

To My Brat:
Kristina Gail

And To My Folks:
Charlotte and Joe

And last, but not least:
Keith Edward Lewis (9/14/1974–3/1/1975)
this book is dedicated to you. My little brother,
whose spirit has hiked with me for thousands of miles.

Adventure with

Introduction

"Hello there, friend. My name is Piney Joe and I come from a long line of families who have lived in southern New Jersey. You could call me a self-professed Pine Barrens Ambassador for I've taken thousands of people on adventures via social media. Just a hundred years ago things were different than they are today. Pineys like me lived awfully close to mother nature, and we learned about flowers, trees, and animals. You know flora and fauna—science stuff. Grandma and Pa always say Math and English are important, but Science is my favorite subject. You say you never heard of Pineys? Other places in the United States that have mountains naturally have Mountain people. In South Jersey, there are the Pinelands and, well, we naturally have Pineys. People living in the area are proud of where they live. Sometimes, you'll hear locals say they live, 'Deep down in the Pines.' And there are all different types of Pineys too."

"What are the Pinelands you ask? That's where our math skills help us! Officially it's a landmass of over 1 million acres declared by the US Congress in 1978 to be the nation's first-ever National Reserve—the New Jersey Pinelands National Reserve. Those 1 million acres also include all the towns and the people that live and work within the

Pinelands National Reserve or Pinelands for short. Maybe you live in one of those towns? Before it became the NJ Pinelands it was called the NJ Pine Barrens. Pine Barrens is an ecological descriptor of the habitat and ecosystem contained within the area. Early settlers said the area was barren because they could not grow typical vegetables, so they began calling it the Pine Barrens.

Today, if you visit you will see it is anything but barren. Heck lest we forget, delicious cranberries and blueberries that everyone loves are grown right here in South Jersey. Farmers are important Pineys too! But we use both names today, Pinelands and Pine Barrens. You could say Pine Barrens is the nickname for the Pinelands National Reserve. Just like if your name was William and all your friends called you Billy!"

There's another type of farmer most people never think of when describing the historical occupations of the Pines. Historians have written about the bog iron industries, including sawmills, furnaces, and forges, which gave way to paper mills and glass factories. But not about this type of farmer who wasn't a real farmer as they owned no land. This type of Piney worked the land and harvested or collected Pineycraft items. That type of Piney is what we call a Woods Piney. Generations of people who lived in the Pine Barrens farmed the woods for items they could sell to the dried flower markets. You see, that is the conundrum for the Piney. These plants had to be harvested in large quantities to make enough money to support themselves and their families and often they would have to venture onto state and federal property to harvest the plants which today is against the law. It wasn't against the law before the Pinelands became a federal reserve in 1978. In essence, the preservation of the New Jersey Pine Barrens turned hundreds of Piney families into outlaws. For most of the time, Woods Pineys did not own the land that they worked. Like the outlaws that robbed banks in the Wild West to earn a living wage, Pineys for a time would risk getting fined or having their vehicles impounded by the law. And many a Piney outlaw took to the woods in modified vehicles and found ways to get into the forest unseen to survive as their families had done for hundreds of years before the land became preserved.

This virtual tour, with Piney Joe as your guide, will show you many of the plants that Pineys collected from different habitats of the New Jersey Pinelands National Reserve, and you'll see for yourself why these plants are so special and why Pineys had their language for plants, and why the people of South Jersey are so proud to be Pineys! You will learn about the history of the plant's name and how to identify it yourself.

You will be surprised that some of these same plants can be found across the United States and probably in your backyard. You might be saying to yourself, "I'll never be able to identify these plants in the wild and what does it matter that we preserve the names of plants the Pineys used? Don't fear, they are relatively common and abundant in the various stops on the Trail Map section of this book. And why should we remember the names of things others used before us? Maybe because if we don't, we are discriminating against the people of the Pines? Native

Americans were the first to suffer from this type of discrimination when their culture and their way of life were systematically erased. The Woods Pineys, like our Native Americans, have become fully assimilated into American culture for better or worse.

We will be heading out into the woods and the woods could be located anywhere in the four corners of the Pinelands National Reserve. It's a hike to nowhere and everywhere at once. And the fully illustrated Trail Map (in the back of the book with key features highlighted to help you get around in the 1.1 million acres of the Pines) will get you going in 0–60 seconds! Who needs an index when you got a trail map right? If you think you've seen it all before, think again. Rediscover with us some things and places that you might have forgotten, or you might have overlooked before.

Let's get the tour with Piney Joe on the road!

Explore the New Jersey Pine Barrens with Piney Joe

Vol I

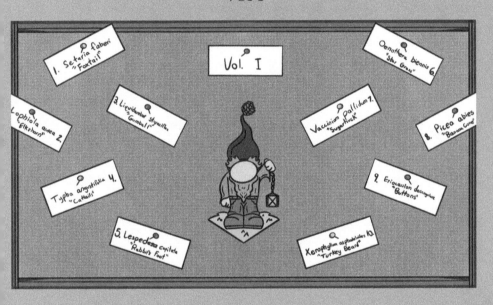

Adventure with

The magic in walking in the woods is unveiled to the trained eye of someone like ole Piney Joe. "Oh, look up ahead on the trail it's a crafty critter, the red fox. Who happens to be one of my friends whom we call Samantha," barked Piney Joe. Before we let Piney Joe go any further let's define what a Piney idiom is and how it relates to each of these images. An idiom as Wikipedia defines it is, "a phrase or expression that typically presents a figurative, non-literal meaning attached to the phrase." Like the saying 'go break a leg' is an idiom and it doesn't mean break a leg, but it does mean 'do a good job or good luck.' These illustrated Piney idioms help you learn the names of Pineycraft plants that Pineys harvested and sold to the dried floral markets.

Standing in the middle of the trailhead Piney Joe taps his foot in impatience, "As I was saying it's no wonder why this plant got its nickname *FOXTAILS*. Look at that big fluffy tail of the Fox. Is it not a marvel?" During the warm months of summer, this plant grows along our roadways and in old farm fields yet to be planted with corn or soybean crops. We know foxes are curious creatures, and it is a curious thing that this plant made its way from East Asia, where it's found in places like Japan, and now can be found in over half of the states in the US.

How would it make you feel if you traveled across an ocean to a new land far away from home? Some plants are brought to our country by the people who lived in the same home country of the plant. We can surmise that they brought something that reminded them of home, making them feel less homesick. In other instances, the seeds of plants that are not naturally occurring were introduced by accident. This Giant Foxtail, or Japanese Bristlegrass, was thought to have arrived in a shipping container from another country in the 1920s. A lonely seed or seeds found their way to shore and to a place to grow.

Newly introduced plants or plants that did not originate here can become invasive. Back in their homeland, these plants evolved with predators that helped maintain the population thus maintaining the balance in the natural web of life. Scientists say the foxtail, when growing in a corn field, can reduce the amount of corn a farmer has to harvest. Other invasive plants or nonnatives can threaten endangered plants by outcompeting them for nutrients in the soil and sunlight, potentially leading our native endangered plants to extinction. It is a very messy thing to understand, but we do know it can cause less diversity in our plant communities.

Ole Piney Joe remembers that in years past both young and old people of South Jersey would pull foxtails one by one adding them up in their hand until they had 50 pieces which made a bunch. These bunches were brought to a dried floral wholesaler and set in hothouses to dry. Remember the farmer is no fan or friend of the foxtails so when the Pineys asked to pull the plants the farmer was happy for their help in controlling the unwanted plant. The brilliant fresh green color we see here with the Fox only fades a little in the drying process after which they were sold to florists and home hobbyists to decorate with. So, some good did come from a plant that many consider a nuisance and a weed. As Ella Wheeler Wilcox, the American author and poet who died in 1919, said, "A weed is but an unloved flower."

Adventure with

J ust round the bend in the trail, Piney Joe espies a white-tail deer. It starts Piney Joe a recollecting. "I remember a time when the mammal elk roamed New Jersey. It is a cousin to the deer you see when out driving with family or like that one that just crossed up ahead. Elk were alive and well, living from New Jersey to Maine up the eastern seaboard. But today sadly they are all gone from most of their early 1800s locations. The Eastern Elk became extinct in New Jersey in 1805. Interesting note: Piney adventurers can travel to Pennsylvania today and see real elk as that state reintroduced the elk to their forest lands in the early 1900s. How cool is that?"

This image of an elk gives you a clue as to what the plant name is that is hand-drawn on the antlers. From one generation to the next, the Pineys always called this plant by this colorful name. Piney Joe reckoned, "If I was to describe to you the plant, I would use my skilled Piney senses. You see this plant in and along waterways in the New Jersey Pine Barrens. It especially can be found in bogs alongside carnivorous plants like Pitcher Plant, Bladder-worts, and various Sundews. This plant is a knee-high green stalked plant. At the very top, the stalks branch out like a set of elk antlers and turn a glossy velvety white. In July, the plant's yellow star-like flowers blossom. This species of plant was first discovered in the NJ Pine Barrens. And another interesting thing about this here plant is it's in a short list of 100 or so plants that make their way up from southern parts of the US and end their distribution in the NJ Pine Barrens. It grows no further north of here."

Did you guess it yet? I bet you did. This plant's common Piney name is **ELKSHORN.** Other people call it Golden-crest because of the golden flowers but we Pineys know it as Elkshorn. For you science fans the Latin Name is Lophiola aurea.

So, if Piney Joe has seen elk roam the New Jersey landscape how old does that make him? And he said, "Short list, short like him right lol?" Piney Joe hollers, "You know I'm more than just a two-foot gnome. I know where there are treasures and I'm not afraid to share it." Even you the reader can see he ain't no two-foot so we gotta watch him as he might be stretching the truth a bit on us here. "Bah either way you're lucky to have me as your guide today. Come tomorrow I'll be back in my garden protecting my treasures. And this here Elkshorn is a real treasure of the Pines I tell ya." So says, Piney Joe.

Now it's your turn to explore and find pictures by searching the following keywords:

- *"Setaria faberi"*
- *"Ella Wheeler Wilcox"*
- *"Lophiola aurea"*

Adventure with

Near where the deer crossed our trail, we enter a small grove of *SWEET GUM* trees or Liquidambar styraciflua. It wasn't too long ago that this was one of America's favorite landscape trees. Known for its 5-pointed star-shaped green leaves that dramatically change in look in the fall months each year. The colors of a gumball machine barely beat it in the number of colors the leaves can be. There are leaves with shades of orange, yellow, red, and purple. Once Mary Treat, one of New Jersey's most famous botanists and authors, gazed upon a Sweet Gum tree that had a parasitic Mistletoe plant growing in it and expressed great emotion for the wellbeing of the Sweet Gum species. In June 1888, Treat wrote, "The Sweet Gum trees, on which it has made its home, have a forlorn, prematurely old look as if they did not enjoy the burden imposed upon them."

"Hey, my long grey beard gives me the same old look as a Sweet Gum tree, but I don't have any Mistletoe growing out of my hat, at least not unless it's close to Christmas," exclaims Piney Joe.

Besides being pleasant to look at, Sweet Gum trees also provide food in their seed pods for many birds. A fun fact is these seed pods from the Sweet Gum tree are a favorite of our NJ state bird, the American Goldfinch. How cool is that? Did you know that fun fact? Bellowing out a big "I did!" Piney Joe says, "I'm more than just an amateur botanist I'm also a birder who knows every species of bird in the Pine Barrens—hundreds reside here part of the time and hundreds more migrate through the Pines each Spring and Fall."

Today the tree has become unpopular in our backyards as the seed pods, or what the Pineys called **GUMBALLS**, can get stuck in the backyard lawn mower and are not fun if you step on them barefooted. Our Piney ancestors would use old onion sacks and collect these gumballs. Florists in the past used these dried brown seed pods in floral decorations that lined many a window scape both in the home and in big city storefronts like New York City and Philadelphia.

Now it's your turn to explore and find pictures by searching keywords:

- *"Mary Treat"*
- *"Mistletoe"*
- *"American Goldfinch"*
- *"Liquidambar styraciflua"*

Adventure with

"Hey, look ahead!" yells Piney Joe. There's a cabin of my hermit friend Wild Tom. As we enter the one-room cabin, we can see hanging on the wall a painting of Tom's cat, and Piney Joe's good friend, Chrissy the Cat. Piney Joe with a tear in his eye moaned, "It might be a little selfish of me to want Chrissy, who once was an outside cat, to stay inside, losing her freedom to roam about, but aren't we all a little selfish sometimes? Let me tell you all about it. Now don't worry, Chrissy the Cat is safe and sound and can be found inside her human's home in South Jersey. She no longer roams the great wide meadows of *CATTAILS* in Lower Bank, New Jersey. One reason for that is it's safer for her to be an inside cat than an outside cat. Too many dangers outside, and Chrissy the Cat can harm wildlife outside like birds and other small animals. Another reason this feline can't adventure in the meadows is because those millions of pencil-thin cattails have all but vanished."

You see plants, like humans and gnomes, need a certain type of environment in which to live. And cattails are tougher than most as they can also take a bit of salt from brackish waters like those along the Mullica River. The New Jersey Pine Barrens are huge and cover many different types of habitats. As we in the Piney Tribe say, "From the Forest Floor to the Salty Shore." Piney Hope Phillips came up with that slogan and it really defines us nicely. But primarily their home is along freshwater ponds and streams. Those meadows at the water's edge have filled in with an imposing imposter. What the scientists call an aggressive invasive species, which we learned about earlier in the section on Foxtails.

Well, don't you know, Phragmites or the Common Reed fits the definition of an invasive for sure. Once Phragmites take seed in an area along a stream, a lake, or a river, it rapidly overcrowds the local plants like cattails. The Woods Piney at one time also harvested Common Reeds alongside cattails. In essence, they were helping to control an invasive species, but that way of life is long gone now. Piney Joe recounts, "One week and one week only in June the banks of rivers like the Mullica would be filled with humans young and old mostly wearing ragged clothing and a pair of "Chuck Converse" sneakers out in the muck using a hand sickle to cut the cattails at the ground level. It was the perfect time to harvest them as the florists used them in flower arrangements and liked them pencil-thin. And they wore those sneakers because they would be wading in the water and once out the shoes would easily dry out. If you waited until July or August to cut cattails, they'd be fat as cigars and tend to blow up! The flower part of the cattail makes a mess when that happens."

But poor Chrissy the Cat's favorite spot to play along the Mullica River no longer exists. Those Cattail meadows were not just good to play in, they also served up many a meal for another river critter, the muskrat, which is a medium-sized rodent. And the wealth of the cattails also helped the Piney families live.

Taking a tour along New Jersey Scenic Byways is one way to visit places like the Mullica River that still exist and once provided habitat for cattails. The state has mapped out a physical route that you can drive that includes the entire diversity of the state. There are eight wonderful Scenic Byways, one aptly named Pine Barrens, that traverses 130 miles of the Pines to include a good portion of the Mullica.

We learned from Chrissy the Cat about plants that come to our hometowns from far away and compete against our local plants for growing space. Now back outside and on the trail again we were just starting to put some mileage behind us when we come upon a wild rabbit posed by the field edge. Fred Flopsy, another one of the woodland friends of Piney Joe, is showing off his cute feet for us to compare to the plant more commonly known as Round-headed Bushclover. Behind him Piney Joe pronounces, "Well, this adorable plant that Fred is sitting next to is what we Pineys call **RABBIT'S FOOT**. It's one of our local plants that must compete with non-native plants too. Sometimes growing up somewhere else has its advantages as there are no local bugs or animals that want to eat you."

Can you see the resemblance in Fred's feet to the green plant that turns brown later in the Fall season? Fred Flopsy doesn't seem to care if he is snuggled up to that rabbit's foot plant or a similar invasive plant like the Chinese Bushclover, Lespedeza cuneata. You see, you can find both along the same trail or in sand pits across the Pine Barrens. Back in the 1990s, when there were still people of the Pine Barrens collecting and selling plants to the dried floral industry, the Chinese version of our Round-headed Clover first started showing up and wasn't a nuisance plant. The problem occurs when you get a non-native that grows and spreads quickly and hogs up the habitat crowding out our local friends. Most Pineys named this Rabbit's Foot, and some called it Brown Burr. I know Fred Flopsy prefers to take his afternoon nap next to rabbit's foot.

Piney Joe questions, "Hey, wait a minute! What's that yellow flower growing alongside the rabbits foot?"

Now it's your turn to explore and find pictures by searching keywords:

- *"Eastern Cottontail Rabbit"*
- *"Lespedeza cuneata"*
- *"Lespedeza capitata"*

Just by looking at that image can you guess this Piney-craft item's common name that was once used in dried floral bouquets? Notice how the artist drew stars on the plant alongside real flowers. "That plant is Evening Primrose or the scientific name Oenothera biennis. Try saying that name out loud twice, lol! What a hoot ha-ha . . . The Pineys of yesterday called this ***STAR GRASS*** or ***BELL GRASS***. Ha-ha so much easier to say out loud. After the plant goes through the beautiful yellow flowering stage of its life, the flowers turn to hard green bell-shaped seed pods. Now you know why some called it Bell Grass," whispered Piney Joe. As Fred Flopsy had just fallen asleep next to the rabbit's foot.

Putting some distance between us and our sleeping friend, Piney Joe goes on about the natural history of Evening Primrose, "The other name, Star Grass, isn't really because the yellow flowers look like stars. Being well versed in the different stages of a plant is akin to some as knowing *woods magic*. Knowing the fall plumage of migrating birds can help you to identify the species of bird seen. And the same bird's plumage in spring, especially the male birds, is usually filled with brilliant colors. Pineys in the 1900s knew *woods magic* or what some call 'aptitude of all things wild.' This is a fancy way of saying they had experience with things around them. Living so close to the plants and animals of the New Jersey Pine Barrens gave them a better understanding of the wild forests."

Evening Primrose goes through growing stages as you and I did from being just tiny babies to who we are today. The Evening Primrose's last stage is to release its seeds for new plants to find a new home and grow up next year. When the green bells turn to brown and crack open releasing seeds, they look like a bursting star, i.e., the name Star Grass.

When you are back home riding through your neighborhood in the late summer months, keep a close eye out your car window. You will eventually spot one of these tall, yellow flowered plants along the roadside. It gets tall and grows in areas that aren't easily mowed, giving it room to live. Here is one more secret tidbit ole Piney Joe knows about this plant, "When you do spy it in the wild, depending on what time of year, look for tiny baby caterpillars of the Primrose Moth (Schinia florida). That moth is a beautiful pink and white with amazing green eyes, just like Piney Joe's seldom seen brilliant green eyes. At dusk and into the early evening hours, you can see this nighttime flyer in and around the plant. Also, if you get a chance, go back to see it later in the Fall which is when Pineys collected it to sell for crafts. Have your parents pick a few pieces and place them in a vase with no water and then you will have some of your very own Piney *woods magic* to gaze at."

Can you imagine anyone ever calling a Piney dumb? So far, we've heard six accounts of different sets of facts that those Woods Pineys knew to make a living in the wild. Tacit knowledge or the "woods knowledge" learned from firsthand experience, not from book learning, was passed on from generation to generation. Pineys lived in harmony with the seasonal rhythm of the land.

There was a time, though, when the word Piney was used in a very mean and derogatory way. In the early 1900s, many different nasty characterizations became popular and were used to describe the people of South Jersey as feeble-minded, degenerate, and worse. The now-debunked science of Dr. Goddard and his assistant Elizabeth Kite stigmatized an entire subpopulation of New Jersey, and it was headline news across the United States that still plagues families today. You can go to your local library and check out the book Dr. Goddard published in 1912 titled *The Kallikak Family: A Study in the Heredity of Feeble-Mindedness.* Their theory was very popular for years and years. Their work was part of the eugenics movement in America and was even imported to Nazi Germany.

It thought that if one of your parents was less than average in certain academics that you too would be less than average. The idea was so popular that they classified people as feebleminded and wanted them to be placed in psychological homes run by the state and prevented from having children of their own for fear of passing on the "dumbness gene." It is crazy to think that even Piney Joe, although he's just a gnome, and individuals like him would fear that one day they would fail a test and because of their different lifestyle and lack of education would lose their freedoms.

Our guide Piney Joe could not put into words what that part of his Piney history meant to him. But he did scoff at the notion, "No city traffic to fight out here. Escaping to the woods is my way of escaping the crazy world we live in! They're the crazy ones, not me. No pressure to do what others want me to do or to be involved in the drama of society. But that poor girl the Doctor used to illustrate his fake theory with. I suppose she never knew her name was not Deborah, for her birth mother called her Emma. The Doctor made up a name for her, Deborah Kallikak. She wasn't born to a family that loved her. No, her only sin was she was born into poverty and was an unwanted child. For she was a beautiful girl and gifted in many things like music and crafts. Just not book smarts. And she never escaped the pseudoscience that labeled her feebleminded, spending her entire life pretty much behind bars after being dropped off at the Training School in Vineland at the age of eight—never to see her mother or father again. I remember her story and will never forget how cruel man must be to keep a woman locked up for 81 years. For her only crime was being different."

Now it's your turn to explore and find pictures by searching keywords:

- *"Oenothera biennis"*
- *"Schinia florida"*
- *"Deborah Kallikak"*

Continuing in solemn silence for quite some time, making our way through the humid woods, the serenity of the place is suddenly disrupted by our guide's growling belly. That tiny thing sure can make loud and strange sounds. "Mmm," Piney Joe smiling exclaims as he reaches down to pick a handful of round glossy blue-looking fruit, "Hey, have you ever had a blueberry? You know that delicious little blue fruit that is packed full of juice and can be found in ice cream, drinks like blueberry lemonade, and especially blueberry pie? Well, there is a special place in the NJ Pine Barrens that is famous for inventing today's blueberry. Oh, I fibbed a little there. Elizabeth White didn't invent the blueberry, as blueberries are a naturally occurring woody plant that grows up and down the East Coast from New Jersey to Maine and across the nation to Washington in a total of 26 states. But New Jersey is in the top 10 producers of commercial blueberries. She had help from botanist Frederick Coville way back then at her dad's farm village called Whitesbog Village in Browns Mills New Jersey."

The year was 1916 when they sold their first cultivated highbush blueberry that was born out of a certain type of wild blueberry or huckleberry bush. Elizabeth White and Frederic Coville share the honor of developing the same blueberry bushes we eat from today. Now I know some Pineys maybe as old as your grandma and grandpa who say that the sweetest blueberries are found growing wild in the Pines on a wild type of plant called huckleberry. A handful of berries popped into the mouth tastes like a mouthful of sugar! That's how this lowbush blueberry plant got its Pineycraft nickname of **SWEETHUCK** or **SUGARHUCK**. Sweet being the berries are the sweetest of all the other kinds of blueberries growing wild in New Jersey. Almost tasting like a mouth full of pure sugar. And Huck being an abbreviation for huckleberry. Isn't that clever of them? Sweethuck home decorations in the shape of hearts and round wreaths hang in families' living rooms across the nation which are made from the branches of the plant species Vaccinium pallidum.

Piney Joe bellows, "Hey, you are forgetting the most important part of the cultivation history of the modern blueberry! Let me tell you that without the collective knowledge of the Piney ole Elizabeth White, queen of the blueberry, would not have been able to develop the modern blueberry for she hired and paid many a Piney family to bring her the largest wild blueberries in South Jersey and to guide her to the bushes themselves. At the time, many different Pineys brought to Mrs. White blueberries, some the size of quarters. One hundred wild blueberry bushes were brought to the farm of Mrs. White and the one that became the mother of all blueberries came from Piney Rube Leek. It was even named after him, 'Rubel', first name followed by the first letter of his last name."

With a bit of Piney Pride, our gnome guide bowed his head. After which he raised it and snickered, "Of course in the Richardson Calendar we sold both sweethuck and hoghuck for the woody plant stems, not for the berries, which was a huge source of income before the cultivated berry came along. One crazy Piney was said to have driven an old beat-up pickup through the woods where no trail or road was just to get deep in the woods to cut a load of these plants. Crazy right? I don't recommend nor condone off-roading in the Pines as vehicles can get hung up or crash, potentially sparking a wildfire or, just as bad for the environment, leaking oil into the very shallow water table below us (think 17 trillion gallons of drinking water below).

Scan to the back of the book to see how to visit the Whitesbog stop on the Piney Joe's Self-Guided Exploration Trail Map and when you go know you'll be visiting the home of the first cultivated blueberry in the world.

"OK, are you ready for another puzzle? The trees up ahead at the road crossing that are on both sides of the trail are a recent introduction to our Pinelands. This item has the funniest name of all. Before I give it away did you know that there is more than just one type of pine tree in the New Jersey Pine Barrens? Wait a minute do you know what a typical Pitch Pine tree looks like? Oh, silly me I bet you do. But do you know what makes a Pine tree and a Pine Forest so neat?" quipped Piney Joe.

"Our Pine Barrens of New Jersey is over 1 million acres. That is a big, big pine forest! And it has all kinds of trees in it. One crazy characteristic about some trees is that when it gets cold, they lose their leaves. I don't know about you, but I put on a wool coat, fuzzy hat, and gloves when it gets cold out. Yet if you look around your backyard in the fall, you'll see trees that are called deciduous trees that lose their leaves. Well jump in your preferred four-wheeled vehicles and take a ride in the Pines of New Jersey in the fall, winter, spring, and summer and you know what you'll see? That's right if you snapped a photo each time in those four visits, you'd see the same evergreen woods. Because pine trees don't lose their leaves which are tiny needles. They stay that same vibrant green all year long! Come to think of it there are more than enough photo subjects to tweet about and retweet about out here in my beloved Pine Barrens!"

There are many types of evergreen pine trees found natively in the Pine Barrens. Like Pitch Pine, Short-leaf Pine, and Virginia Pine. Alongside these evergreen trees is another evergreen tree that has been introduced to the US from Europe. The colorful image of this tree, with what appears to be yellow bananas growing on it, is a Norway Spruce. Those yellow bananas are a hint to its Piney nickname.

The Pineys in New Jersey didn't seek this tree out for its wood, but its banana-like cone. Isn't that one of the silliest names for a pinecone aka ***BANANA CONE***? Did you know that the cones of pine trees contain the seeds of the tree that could one day grow from the forest floor and reach the sky? The seeds are indeed in the protective cones. You and I are like seeds of our family. Our family forms a protective cone around us to make sure we too one day grow big and tall and reach for the sky! But on occasion, Piney Joe and his friends have been known to use banana cones in a different sense. Both the new green cones and the lighter and older brown cones that look like bananas also make great projectiles and when beamed at a friend certainly can leave a mark!

Piney Joe mutters, "We best keep moving. We are only nearing the halfway mark before we have to loop back."

Now it's your turn to explore and find pictures by searching keywords:

- *"Elizabeth C. White"*
- *"Frederick Coville"*
- *"Vaccinium pallidum"*
- *"Pitch Pine"*
- *"Norway Spruce"*

Nearing a wayward bog that seems to be lined with a white flower to the left, Piney Joe calls out, "It's funny to a Piney gnome that there is such an invention as a button. I guess you humans need buttons for your clothes, but not me! If I wore buttons, I'd probably get caught in a sticky briar patch out along a cranberry bog and be helpless until a farmer came along and freed me. No thank you! You keep your buttons as I don't need them slowing me down when I'm out adventuring in a Pine Barrens bog like this one here. Although I hike with a backpack most of the time when exploring to store my water hydroflask in."

And that's the same place you'll see this plant—bogs, and wet areas throughout the woods. You see this plant has several sister plants that all have the same white button-looking flower top. They all can be found at different times of the year growing in similar habitats and the botanist people call the family of plants Pipeworts. Botanist is a funny name—just as funny as calling this plant **BUTTONS**, ha-ha! So, you know, botanists are experts or students who study plants. Only one type or species of this plant can be said to have been collected by Piney families out in those soggy boggy places. Its formal name used by botanists is Eriocaulon decangulare.

Why do you think it is better to use the formal name the botanists use than a common name like Buttons? For one, only the Piney people use the term Buttons. Another reason is every plant and animal has a formal name and if everyone uses the same agreed-upon name, then it's easier to communicate. If my parents call me Piney Joe and I tell everyone my name is Piney Bob. Well, when I'm at a picnic with my folks and a friend calls me Piney Bob my parents will be confused about whom my friend is talking to. That's why we use formal names or scientific names like Eriocaulon decangulare to avoid confusion.

But shouldn't we also remember the names of plants that both Native Americans and our own Piney brethren used? Remember, changing the name of something breaks the connection of the people who knew it by that name only and stories are lost that were interwoven within their culture. Native Americans used many of these plants first for medicine and or as a food source. Many of the Pineycraft items that Pineys harvested were common plants that surely local natives shared the first knowledge of with European settlers in South Jersey. If anything, we can voice a thank you to those before us who have given to our community's lexicon so much.

Take a minute and look at the back of this book. There you will find an index that lists three names for each plant species mentioned in the text. In alphabetical order, there is the common name, Piney name, and Latin or scientific name.

Now it's your turn to explore and find pictures by searching keywords:

- *"Pipeworts"*
- *"Eriocaulon decangulare"*

Adventure with

S tanding straight up and removing the lean in his stance, Piney Joe starts the walk to the turn in the trail that will begin to loop us back to the parking area.

"Mmm, did I ask you how old you were when we first started this journey together? Now that we've come this far, I guess you could say we are friends now. And it wouldn't be rude to ask you your age, right? Oh well, it doesn't matter as I know by now you are old enough to wonder why you have a Piney gnome as a guide, yet you are young enough to believe that maybe gnomes and such a thing as *woods magic* exist. That's what we Pineys collectively recognize as the energy and passing of time that travels through all living things in our woods. We who experience it are said to be in the *Know*. Meaning we know something that someone else doesn't know or that someone else ignores."

Piney Joe held for a minute in his forward momentum waiting to hear his group's response. "I reckon any answer other than 'Yes' would have you failing my test and we both can agree that Piney gnomes exist otherwise you'd have to find your way back to the car on your own!" yelped Piney Joe.

To our unvoiced answers, Piney Joe replied, "You see you might have said you were all of just eight years of age, or you might be reading this book and be an oldy and have had thirty cake days already. At either age your parents watched you grow year after year. We all go through growth spurts physically, and sometimes both physical and emotional life stages. It is the same with plants in the woods. Sometimes those stages are so dramatic you don't recognize the plant after it goes from birth to seed. That long-winded discussion we just had aptly applies to this here patch along the trail. Those plants right there are everybody's favorite pinelands species. [Piney Joe points to the nearby tall green grass with what looks like a white easter flower sticking five inches above Piney Joe's pinecone topped hat.] You can find them especially in recently burnt off pinewoods as they are successional plants. *Successional* means one of the first to resprout in an area affected by fire. Can you guess its Piney name? It's **TURKEYBEARD**."

Our guide continues, "Many a Piney knows that it takes woods smarts to recognize the various ways *woods magic* transforms this brilliant white flowery wonder into an upside-down 'J' curled stalk. But it's the upside-down J curled brown stalk that it takes its common name from, Turkeybeard. And Pineys only harvested the plant in its dried brown stage months after its white flower appeared. Our botanist friends call it by its scientific name Xerophyllum asphodeloides. Ha-ha, say that twice! My gnome tongue gets tied every time I try to say it. Whoosh what a mouth full. My Piney brethren's name reflects the transformation the plant goes through with a bit of that *woods magic*. After the white flower turns brown it curls into the shape of an upside-down J resembling the male turkey's beard. Get an adult to Google 'male turkeybeard.' It's a funny thing. Well, funny, to a gnome. Not so funny if you are a turkey."

Speaking of beards. Did you know a full beard like Piney Joe's or the Turkeybeard shown here was unheard of in the original inhabitants of South Jersey, the Lenape Indians? Piney Joe blurts out, "Way back when, before there were Pineys in those days of early life in the Pines, the Lenape men supposedly plucked out any facial hair using a clam shell-like tweezers. I guess you could say it was the easiest way to keep clean-shaven and at the same time stay 'On Fleek.' You know I have many teenage cousins who wish they could grow a beard as fast and long as this here plant Turkeybeard yet alone [hands stroking his long beard] one as I have."

In case you were wondering how a country bumpkin like Piney Joe knows the word "Fleek," let's respond to your unvoiced question, lol. It's because one of the quirkiest things about the New Jersey Pine Barrens is its geographic location. Being nearly centered on one side of a hand-drawn triangle on a map between two major cities: New York City and Philadelphia. So naturally, there is an influx of people and ideas, which is a good thing, just ask Piney Joe. Piney Joe enthusiastically answers, "My friend Joe taught me the word as he uses it all the time. He's the singer of the band Jackson Pines and lives near Manayunk in Philly. They got this one song called "(Never Gonna) Bury Me," which I heard live, that mentions 'Scatter it all through the pines. . . Bury my name in a history book. . .' It's great. Everything about the Pine Barrens has been influenced by people coming and going through the area, to and fro. Just on our short walk, you probably can feel the energy draw these woods have for so many people. Our music and our culture are influenced by visitors, and we influence and inspire those visitors as well. And as I've shown here along our hike, these ten different Pineycraft plants helped Piney families sustain their way of life by them selling the harvested plants ultimately to the big city floral markets of NYC and Philly. It's good to be a Piney!"

Now it's your turn to explore and find pictures by searching keywords:

- *"Xerophyllum asphodeloides"*
- *"Lenape Indians"*

PLANT LIST OF PINEY JOE'S ADVENTURE
(in sequential order)

*Native and non-native plants were harvested as part of the Richardson Calendar

1.   *FOXTAIL* aka Setaria faberi
2.   *ELKSHORN* aka Lophiola aurea
3.   *GUMBALL* aka Liquidambar styraciflua
4.   *CATTAILS* aka Typha angustifolia
5.   *RABBIT'S FOOT* aka Lespedeza capitata
6.   *STAR GRASS* or *BELL GRASS* aka Oenothera biennis
7.   *SWEETHUCK* or *SUGARHUCK* aka Vaccinium pallidum
8.   *BANANA CONE* aka Picea abies
9.   *BUTTONS* aka Eriocaulon decangulare
10.   *TURKEYBEARD* aka Xerophyllum asphodeloides

It looks like a poet by the name of Lillian Arnold Lopez in 1982 wrote "The Pine Gnome" about a close relative to Piney Joe. So, we thought we'd share a tidbit of the poem here. It's a rhyming story with drawings from Lilli Lopez which she dedicated to her granddaughters Melanie, Valerie, Melissa, Marissa, and Alisha. *Credit Anita Marie Lopez.*

THE PINE GNOME

In the heart of the Barrens dwelt a little Pine Gnome;
    he seldom strayed far from his toadstool home.
Tho, when duty called, this little Gnome rode --
    over woodstrails on his steed, Tippy Toad.
Now, gnomes are guardians of treasures on earth;
    gold, silver, and diamonds, and gems of great worth.
Well, flora and fauna are Pine Barren's treasure,
    to protect it, as such, was our little Gnome's pleasure.

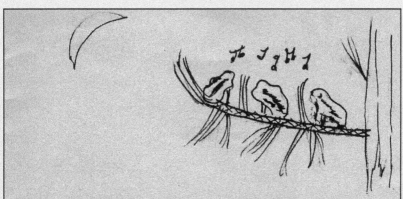

The Gull, tenderhearted and wise, coaxed a smile;
    said, "For hundreds of years you have not shirked your duty;
Well, we all need a holiday once in awhile;
    it takes leaving home, sometimes, to realize its beauty."

The sun was just setting, as homeward they flew;
    a most radiant sight, and the Gnome's face was, too.

That night as he slept by the song of tree frogs;
    he dreamt of rare treasures that grew near his home;
Like 'sapphires' in swamps, and 'rubies' in bogs;
    and you never could find a more blissful Pine Gnome.

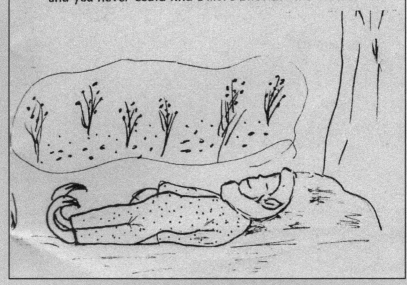

Now it's your turn to explore and find pictures by searching keywords:

- *"Sapphires in swamps" aka Blueberries or Vaccinium corymbosum*
- *"Rubies in bogs" aka Cranberries or Vaccinium macrocarpon*

Explore the New Jersey Pine Barrens with Piney Joe

Vol II

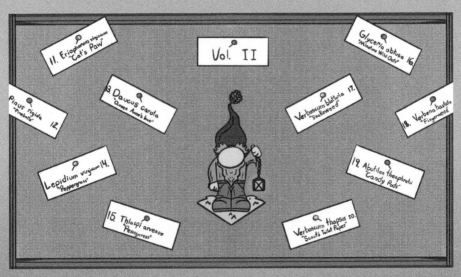

Adventure with

In this second volume, we continue to explore the New Jersey Pine Barrens and the folklore surrounding Pineys—the people of the Pine Barrens. Topics include why plants can be good and bad for the environment in a nonthreatening way (alien vs native plants) and the importance of both local and scientific names of plants. We help identify ten more common pineycraft plants and trees found in South Jersey with our guide—Piney Joe the Gnome.

This knowledge can teach us, humans, to appreciate the environment and local history. It builds connection and respect for the land and people that, hopefully, will deter future bad behaviors which plague the federal Pinelands National Reserve today—behaviors such as littering or off-road destruction in the 56 different Pinelands communities.

It's a fact that gnomes don't exist—or do they? Piney Joe, a Piney gnome, does a great job of helping us explore the New Jersey Pine Barrens and with a little help from the hand-drawn images of ten Piney idioms you'll be better equipped to explore the Pine Barrens on your own. Just maybe along the way you will have formulated your own opinion of what it is to be a Piney and dispelled the notion that Pineys are all backwoods folks. As Piney Joe says himself, "My purpose, the one I derive the most meaning from in life, is having the ability to show visitors a different image of my home and to keep fighting the image Dr. Goddard painted of the people of the pines. Piney Lives Matter."

Stopped in the middle of the trail, Piney Joe scratching his head questions, "Did you see that cat's paw back there near the *BUTTONS*?"

Proper naming conventions or nomenclature is serious business. Take for instance this plant. Piney Joe gave away its Piney name already, *CAT'S PAW*. It is more commonly known to plant hobbyists or amateur botanists as Tawny Cottongrass. This plant also goes by the scientific name of Eriophorum virginicum. So that's three names. One pineycraft name, then the more commonly known local name, and finally the Latin name or scientific name. As botanist Chris Benda, better known by his social media moniker the Illinois Botanizer, can tell you it gets quite confusing. Mr. Benda says, "While easier for laypeople to understand, common names are often botanically incorrect. Many plants we call rushes are technically sedges. Common names such as Tawny Cottongrass, which is a sedge, Broomsedge, which is a grass, Woolgrass, which is a sedge, or Peppergrass (actually mustard), and Canada Thistle (from Europe, not Canada) make the point that while difficult to spell and pronounce, botanical names are more useful for communicating the names of plants." You see it is serious business!

You are lucky to have Piney Joe as a guide. For Piney Joe can translate the various names of these pineycraft plants and in a group of people with one botanist, one piney, and one tourist he can give all three names, and everyone will understand what he's pointing out in a bog alongside the road in Chatsworth or anywhere there are lowland bogs in the Pine Barrens. And Pineys like him have been hired and paid good money by the greatest scientists of our time to help find rare plants and animals of the Pine Barrens. For who else knows the land as well as the people who live in the area? You know, that raises a good question about where Pineys kept all that money received for services rendered back then as the international plant community and its botanists discovered with great interest our beloved Pine Barrens? Let's ask Piney Joe.

Piney Joe, leaning against a Bull Pine, the only tree in the clearing in this section of the trail, answered with a chuckle, "That reminds me of a story my friend ole Piney Judd told me just last week. Let's see if I can retell it without cracking up myself. As Judd said to me with his Chatsworthian slang, 'There was this olde couple named Buster (Elvin) & El-C (Elsie) Leek. Buster, born in 1902, always saved his money at home and didn't trust banks. He used to put his money in the old cook stove because Elsie, born in 1905, never baked or used the oven part. Well, one day Elsie decided to bake something or to use the stove not knowing Buster hid his money there. Up in smoke went all his savings. And it was quite a bit and when the Chatsworth couple went to the closest bank being in Mount Holly, they were told they couldn't help them with the half-burnt paper money.' To answer your question, the Pineys were creative when it came to saving money, lol. And there was distrust in things

outside their community that was fostered by the perpet-
uated false stories of the degenerate Pineys."

Now it's your turn to explore and find pictures by searching keywords:

- *"Eriophorum virginicum"*
- *"Laypeople"*

Adventure with

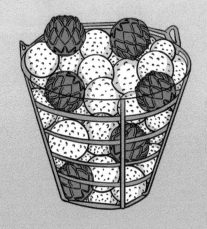

If you were to ask any person what the symbol of the New Jersey Pine Barrens is, the top answer to that question would be Pinecones or the Pine tree. The four types of pine trees commonly found in the Pine Barrens landscape are Pitch Pine, like the old Bull Pine Piney Joe was leaning up against, Short-leaf Pine, Virginia Pine, and the introduced Eastern White Pine. There's one tree above all the rest that is tops to Piney Joe. "I am the most popular gnome of the Pines and have to keep up my reputation. There's one thing I do while looking in the mirror each morning. And that's to straighten my Pinus rigida or more commonly called Pitch pinecone on my hat." The pinecone on top of Piney Joe's cone-shaped hat is often mistaken for a ball. See the image of a wire basket full to the rim mixed with golf balls and pinecones or **PINEBALLS**.

Now how do you suppose Piney Joe got that favorite pinecone of his being so vertically challenged himself? There are several areas in South Jersey that are home to the pygmy pines which are unusually stunted Pitch Pines—officially called the Pygmy Pine Plains. Trees are sometimes also called dwarves for their maximum height is mostly four feet. So, if you're tall, say six feet (poor Piney Joe is but fifteen inches) you can gaze out across the plains, and nothing will obstruct your view. Piney Joe interjects, "We in South Jersey are more civilized and don't call our pines dwarves but did you know those New Yorkers who have their version of our Pine Barrens just a wee bit smaller in total acreage have a place in Long Island's Suffolk County called Dwarf Pine Plains. Bet you didn't know that didja?"

Not too long ago you may have seen a person or two out in those areas. But what would they be doing out there on the Plains? Did you know that the people of the Pine Barrens have for generations collected the pinecones from the Pygmy Pine Plains of Warren Grove? It's true and now you know! Pineys of old would pull the pinecones using gloves, as the pinecones are prickly to the touch. Hazards of pineballing, besides scratching up your hands, were a misplaced step on a rattlesnake or placing your hand on what some call a Cow Killer which is a Red Velvet ant. And then you had to dodge death from above from the active military bombing range.

Many long days were spent walking from pine bush to pine bush collecting buckets of brown cones which were then put into bags that held exactly 1000 cones. They would be able to sell the closed cones to florists and wholesale dried floral businesses, thus earning a living wage. One fun fact is that the people who purchased the cones had to artificially open the cones as Pitch Pine trees have a unique relationship with forest fires. You see, a forest fire helps the Pitch Pines by removing competition from oak trees. If you were able to heat a closed pinecone several hundred degrees, it would open just like it naturally does after a forest fire to reseed the forest floor.

Jokingly Piney Joe says, "When I was little—now don't go saying anything rude about my height and me being short. It is what it is. As I was saying, in my younger days, maybe when I was a teenager, me and my woods friends would walk the white sand roads that crisscross the Plains, or we'd hop onto an abandoned railroad track and just start walking. Just hanging out and doing nothing much other than talking, but just being out here was good enough for us. This and that could be the name of a photography exhibit of all the odd things you find in the Pines. There's always something new to discover. Heck, photographers have tons of stuff to shoot out here. You got the long straight white sand roads that contrast so beautifully with the evergreen pine trees and there are sand pits here and there. I and my friends loved to find old sand pits carved out of the landscape where you could find some interesting things. They say Jimmy Hoffa and other mob hits are buried out in the Pines."

There's no real evidence that Hoffa, or anyone else for that matter. is buried out in the Pines. It's strictly anecdotal evidence. So, no real proof of such claims, but the abandoned and burnt vehicles that litter the sand pits and many a forgotten road sure do seem to heighten the probability of illegal activity.

Hey, Piney Joe, quit fidgeting with your pinecone on your hat, and let's get the tour going again! Piney Joe grumbles, "I'll be darned if I'm gonna walk around looking like a darn fool 'cause my pineball is crooked. You try to live all your life only fifteen inches tall! And sometimes you know when I'm remembering the old days and old times, I get emotional. Some say the Piney culture is lost. I remember and if I tell you about it you will remember, and nothing will be lost but good friends whose travels on Earth have expired. Just thinking of seeing a Piney out there on the Plains sticking out like a sore thumb among the green foliage brings a tear to my eye. But it ain't lost! There are still Woods Pineys out there practicing old traditions and each of you touring the pines with me won't forget us Pineys right?"

Here we'll start looping back to the start of our trek. This portion of the loop is shorter than the rest by a tad.

Now it's your turn to explore and find pictures by searching keywords:

- *"Dwarf Pine Plains"*
- *"Pygmy Pine Plains"*

Adventure with

Our guide likes to tell friends jokingly that he's the "King of the Pineys," being in a direct line to the king of England. You already know from your early school studies in history that America was once full of colonies of England and under the rule of the English monarchy, right? There were thirteen colonies including New Jersey, which was first founded under King Charles. Eventually, with the Declaration of Independence in 1776, the colonies broke away from the rule of then King George III. Well, the story goes that there were people who settled in the remote Pine Barrens to escape persecution for being loyal to the crown during America's revolt. Perhaps this is just a yarn, but one that even Piney Joe likes to spin along with other living residents of South Jersey.

"Can a King or Queen also be a farmer? You know other families worked in tough Pine Barrens industries like bog-iron or worked in tree cutting outfits or sawmills. And I'm not talking about my bloodline being from high English stock. That's because today we wave the American flag and my loyalties lie with America. I mean a different kind of King and Queen. Just look at the history of Batsto Village in Hammonton, New Jersey. I'd say old Charles Read who created the Batsto Iron Works in 1766 alongside the Batsto River was the first king of the Bog Iron industry. Successive families took the monarchy over the years like the Reads,

Coxes, and Richards. The end of that monarchy was the death of a good friend to the Piney, ole Joseph Wharton way back in 1909. And lest we forget, the delicious cranberries and blueberries that are grown in South Jersey are also Pine Barren's industries. Farmers are important Pineys too! And I'm King of the Woods Pineys who farmed pineycrafts, supplying the dried floral industry that didn't end until the early 1990s. So, we outlasted almost all the other traditional Pine Barrens industries, all but the tasty blueberry and cranberry industries."

Knowing the background of some Pineys who claimed to be close relations with the English monarchy, could the Piney name of this plant have been given as a nod to Queen Anne of England? Her position was three rulers before George III who lost all control of the newly founded United States of America. *QUEEN ANNE'S LACE* has a bloody purple-red pin drop in the center, maybe foreshadowing of the blood shed to come on American soil.

Piney Joe, like many other Pineys, considers the elegant white crown of this summer biennial plant to be a welcome sight along the roads of the Pines. The remoteness to the area helps to define the people, and their names for plants connects them to history. Even though it is forgotten who gave this plant its common name of Queen Anne's Lace, each new plant connects the people who remember the name to New Jersey's past. Being a common plant it's not hard to see how it made its way from the field edge to the country home's vase that adorns the dining room table of many families. Oh, and even the Pineys only use the common name of Queen Anne's Lace for this plant. It's a type of wild carrot but mostly botanist folks only care to know that factoid.

Now it's your turn to explore and find pictures by searching keywords:

- *"Batsto Iron Works"*
- *"Queen Anne's Lace"*

Adventure with

Up ahead on the trail we see another Pineycraft item worthy of pause in our hike. Piney Joe points and calls out, "Speaking of the dining room tables and the mouth-watering dishes that sustain our bodies. Can you guess the name derived from carefully reviewing this plant's image? More and more people are finding ways to subsist off the land and looking towards the old ways to live. There are plants that many call weeds or unwanted plants. But a weed to you may be a treasured guest to another." Piney Joe himself has partaken of the natural seasoning of this plant, topped on a tomato sandwich with great satisfaction.

Being one of two species found commonly in overgrown farm fields or disturbed urban areas, this plant was once part of the dried floral industry where Piney families would harvest the plant in the early summer months. A day spent in an open field pulling this deep-rooted plant out of the dried and rock-hard soil was a tiring job. But it was often rewarding as the plant was sold by the pound. Later it was dried and used in floral arrangements that aged little even after years and years of being part of someone's home decor.

"There's a story that gets taller and taller each time I tell it," Piney Joe laughs. "So, one of the greatest of all time friends to the Woods Piney and the most famous proprietor of Pineycraft items was John Richardson. He had at one time owned a horse racetrack in Mount Holly, New Jersey, and many a story of raucous high stakes poker games is told, with betting on the horses there among Richardson's Pineycraft business. Later in life, he lived on a farm in Wrightstown, New Jersey. This is where the tall tale starts. You see this plant we see there along the trail was sold by the pound. There was a sycamore tree that had to be the biggest in the county and one of the oldest growing there alongside the 1700s farmhouse John Richardson lived in. Hanging from that shade tree was a metal feed bag scale with a dangling hook below. That's where the Piney would hook the bale of weeds and determine how heavy the bale was and how many total pounds were to be paid out. Well in that old gnarly tree 25 feet up was a rusty, black-handled machete. The tall tale is that the original owner of the farm butchered chickens at the tree and left his knife in the young tree's crook. How it rested there, year after year, never be seen and recovered by anyone is beyond me."

If you guessed **PEPPERGRASS** or Poor Man's pepper, "Hot diggity you got it right." So many of these wild plants that Pineys collected as part of the Richardson Calendar have functioned as medicinal and or edible parts of our existence. Remember the Richardson Calendar refers to the Piney list of plants that were harvested from the Pine Barrens and surrounding areas each month of the year supplying the dried floral industry. Do you ever go for a walk at a state park in the Pines, say Wharton or Brendan T. Byrne? It's easy to spot Peppergrass growing along a parking lot at one of these properties. Remember it's a living thing connecting you to the history of the area. History doesn't always reside in a book or a museum. You and Piney Joe are living history too! Again, you can find these Pineycraft plants throughout the Pine Barrens and when you reach down and touch the plant, well, you're connecting with the people and history of the place. Do you know? So go out and be confident and share your knowledge. Because Piney Tribe Knows.

"Ok, Let's get moving as just a few hundred feet ahead is a steep hill to climb and when we get to the top, we can climb a fire tower!" exclaims Piney Joe.

Special note of concern or warning to never consume plants that have not been properly identified by an expert.

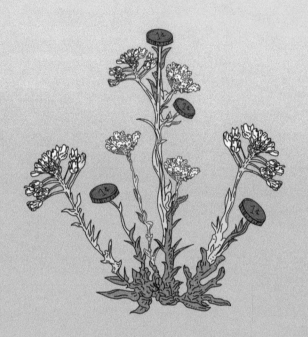

By now if you've made it on this adventure this far with Piney Joe, you might be asking yourself why there are so many plants that people collect and decorate their homes with? What's the history behind a wreath made from this plant featured here that seems to have copper pennies growing out of it? Piney Joe can tell you that it's another plant found in old fallow farm fields and along the roadways of the Pines like Peppergrass. It's similar in fashion to the other plants of the Richardson Calendar and was gathered in abundance to supply the florist trade. But when did we as a species homo sapien begin decorating our homes with wreaths before it was a million-dollar industry with television stars like Martha Stewart showcasing home fashions for America?

Much of the history of the dried floral industry can be summarized in one sentence, "A plant that is immortal or everlasting keeping its shape and colors for years to come." Piney Joe himself being a gnome of good nature (and good size in the belly, lol) is immortal. There are certain plants that when dried will shatter and go to pieces. Plants that don't are classified as Immortelles or Everlastings. For a long time, we humans have been using flowers and plants in other ways besides as a food source. There is evidence that flowers have been used at funerals of loved ones since we were Neanderthals. Ancient cultures like the Egyptians,

Greeks, and Romans were using them for funerals and as part of the daily wardrobe. It's said that our modern wreath comes from the Roman Empire where various levels of government officials wore crowns of specific plants that displayed their position in society.

Sweating from the steady climb to the patch of **PENNY-CREST** atop the hill growing at the foot of the fire tower, Piney Joe considers, "There's nothing basic about the 100-foot fire towers in our Pinelands. Besides giving a great view, they also serve a critical purpose in wildfire prevention as many early alerts come from expert fire spotters stationed on one of these towers. Rangers are sometimes stationed on these towers eight hours a day scanning the horizon for smoke. The Adirondack mountains also have a fire tower network for the same purpose in upstate New York. Let's climb to the top and back down with Yeet!"

Most of the fire towers in the New Jersey Pine Barrens are fenced off and require a ranger's permit to climb. Here either we stumbled upon a fire tower that had a ranger in attendance, who was kind enough to allow us to safely climb to the top, or we found one of the few that are unmanned but still accessible to the public, like the tower at Brendan T. Byrne. (*See in the back of the book—Piney Joe's Self-Guided Exploration Trail Map.*)

Were you able to guess the common Piney name from this plant's Piney idiom? Its Piney name is Pennycrest, though it is more commonly known to plant enthusiasts as Field Pennycress. Many call this a nuisance plant, since it is a non-native plant from Europe, but it has provided much-needed income to hundreds of Piney families over the years. We know some plants have found their way to North America and are now simply transplants similar to someone moving to the Pine Barrens from Philadelphia. Native plants vs. non-natives made no difference to the Richardson Calendar or to the Pineys who harvested it in the spring months of April and May. Another fun fact about Pennycrest, aka Field Pennycress, is that within the last century scientists have found the weed to be a great source of biofuel. So, one day the oil from this plant could be powering a jet you're flying on.

As we catch our breath from climbing up and racing down the fire tower with Piney Joe, it gives us a chance to think about what Piney Joe had said earlier.

Piney Joe said his favorite school subject was Science, but his Ma & Pa reminded him that Math and English were also important. Well, add to that list of classes Geography. Now the geography lesson, or more importantly the distribution of plants geographically, straight from Piney Joe's mouth to your ears: "You see there's more to learn from some plants than others. There's one that teaches human history, but it also teaches land history. A wetland plant species, its geographic distribution across the US is limited to the East Coast within states that touch the Atlantic Ocean, all but Georgia and Florida." Piney Joe scoffs, "I wonder why it doesn't live in Florida? I'm even tempted to retire to Florida and make my residence near some of my distant relatives, those dwarves of Snow White's. I bet you didn't know that Snow White's house is in Port Orange, Florida? I kid you not."

Another wonderfully illustrated Piney idiom is labeled with the word "Oats." Geographically speaking, this plant sticks to water. Pineys called this plant *MINIATURE WILD OATS* but again it's more commonly known as Blunt Managrass. Pineys see things in simple terms and this plant's flower spikelets clumped at the top looked much like the wild oats of your breakfast cereal oatmeal. A good bowl of oatmeal probably powered many a Piney as they prepared to harvest this plant at the close of August and early September when the air begins to take a chill with the oncoming of fall. And many a Piney has some blood mixed in them of the original Quaker settlers to the region. You've probably heard of William Penn the founder of the state of Pennsylvania, right? He was a famous person of the Quaker faith. So that's how this Pineycraft got its name.

You know another wicked cool thing about the Geography of the Pines is not what's on top of the land per se but what resides below only a few feet in some instances. Underneath there is an aquifer that provides 17.7 trillion gallons of water to South Jersey, the Kirkwood-Cohansey aquifer. And because the cedar creeks are fed by the aquifers or spring-fed, they are always at perfect cool temperatures. These amber creeks have Miniature Wild Oats dotting their banks. Water pollution is always a major concern in the Pine Barrens because the water table is always so close below the surface of the sand that acts as its filter. Illegal dumping and overconsumption are major issues.

Echoing this sentiment, Piney Joe regards, "One of my jobs as an ambassador of the Pines is to also be a protector of the Pines. I don't wear a red hat like my gnome cousins for I don a green hat and green attire. Why do you ask? Because I can go unseen in the woods, and when I do witness illegal dumping or other unlawful acts in the Pine Barrens, I can then call in a report to the New Jersey Department of Environmental Protection (NJDEP). Sometimes things don't make sense to me. Like when you see construction debris littered at the periphery of a dirt road in the Pines. It confuses me as to why anyone would do that, you know? But I always help by reporting it when I find it because I remember I'm an ambassador of the Pines. *IF* you respect the land, you are an ambassador to the Pines as well. Our authorities have so much area to cover as the saying goes, "Piney Tribe from the Forest Floor to the Salty Shores." I know I'm a Piney from my nose down to my hiney. And I'm proud of it and to be proud you must respect the land above all else. And I'm doing my part to keep it clean."

Now it's your turn to explore and find pictures by searching keywords:

- *"Poor Man's Pepper"*
- *"Field Pennycress"*
- *"Blunt Managrass"*

We continue down the hill heading east on our return leg of the trip. Piney Joe must be warming up to the group as he articulates, "Hopefully this has been a very informative hike as I know you guys have been great listeners. My best words of advice to folks that I meet along life's trail is to be you, you know? It's hard trying to be someone else every day. I'd have to put on a baseball cap or something funny like it to change my appearance to be like someone else. But being me is freeing. I'm a Piney gnome. I can goof off and go on hikes with you guys or I can sit on top of grassy gnoll among red-topped mushrooms and be my introverted self in peace."

He continues in a questioning tone, "What kind of guide would I be if this here Piney gnome didn't give you a few words of caution about hiking in the Pine Barrens? First off, did you know there are 23 species of snakes in New Jersey? Nearly all of them except for Copperhead, Northern Ribbon snake, and Smooth Green, which are only found in the North, and the Queen snake, which is believed to be extirpated, can be found in the Pine Barrens. Everyone knows 'Piney Tribe Brakes For Snakes' as they serve a vital role in the environment consuming insects and rodents and are part of the food chain for other animals. They deserve protection even if they are the most misunderstood creature of the animal kingdom. Only one of our snakes, the Eastern Timber Rattlesnake, is venomous and it's best to give it room when encountering it in the Pines like any wild animal. Nearly all snakes can and will bite in defense."

Piney Joe himself has escorted plenty of snakes across highways in the Pines so that they would not be run over by cars. For snakes are at the top of the list of his woodland friends. And snakes have been friends to many Piney families as well. There ahead at the road crossing of our trail we see the power line crossing is filled with **SNAKE-WEED**. That's another Pineycraft item that was cut with a sickle and sold by the pound to the dried floral industry in America. There in the middle is Piney Joe's friend Sammy, an eastern (black) snake. Everyone knows the Rattlesnake makes a rattle with its tail but so do many other snakes. And the seed pod on the top of this plant, Verbascum blattaria, after it is done blossoming and dries out, makes a rattling sound too. Which gives it its Piney name of Snakeweed.

Piney Joe alleges, "Out of all my friends the black snake is treated the worst. Maybe he gets labled as such because he just looks scary (which is just plain ignorance) or maybe because other members of his family are known to be dangerous. But his diet of eating rodents is a much-needed service we all can thank him for. I don't judge a plant by the type of flower it shows. A plant is a plant and as such each serves a purpose like you and me do and each of us and them are beautiful. Come to think of it, if you are casting judgment, you are looking for negative things. Even my friend the sly fox Samantha occasionally steals a chicken to eat from a nearby farmer. I steal a bit of honey from the honeybees when I can find their hive. But Sammy and

Samantha are good friends of mine. And each of us is good in our way. They might be a ragtag bunch, but we come from all walks of life, and I wouldn't have it any other way."

After passing over the powerline cut in the trail we continue into the forest where the sun is blocked out by the thick canopy of Mountain Laurel on all sides of the trail. The evergreen laurel formed a tunnel over our walking trail. Then it happened!

There in the dim light, Piney Joe yowled, "Did you hear that?" [Pausing for effect.] "Why I bet that screech was none other than Mrs. Leeds' abandoned 13th child, Mr. Jersey Devil himself dontcha know. Howling of the baby devil or the sound of a baby wailing sometimes can be heard when out collecting Pineycraft items or traipsing through the woods like we are out in the middle of nowhere. Remember when exploring in the Pine Barrens the middle of nowhere probably once was a 'somewhere' to someone or something. You gotta expect the unexpected. Stories have been told of Pineys finding unmarked graves in the pines or encountering strangely placed memorial stones and weird shrines deep in the Pines. And I believed I saw a coyote dart across my path and dangling from its mouth was the bones of a human hand. Maybe dug out of an old, unmarked grave from one of the many ghost towns in the Pines from bygone industries? Whose to tell. Heck, that noise we just heard was probably more likely the crying of a coyote pup than ole Mr. JD in the flesh."

Markedly picking up the pace, we eventually breach the laurel tunnel, and the woods open back up now, walking along with an old blueberry patch in the direction of our car and safety.

Many miles of trail and dirt roads are to be explored in the 1.1 million acre national reserve. Some remote sites are in the loneliest parts of the forest and the countryside can be unforgiving. When hiking alone one moment you can feel the sun on your face and the butterflies flying around your head and the next your mind is playing tricks on you and you're again thinking about the Jersey Devil and what tree he's hiding behind. One could suffer an anxiety attack or break down and cry from the freakish period of silence that occurs when one's mind wanders to the "what ifs."

Piney Joe retorts, "Now trust me when I say I've suffered my identity crisis in that sort of state of mind. You know the 'what ifs'; what if I break a leg deep out in the middle of nowhere or what if I run into a pack of wild creatures being driven on by the madder-than-hell Jersey Devil? Ain't I who I say I am? Where'd all my confidence go? A tough ole Piney gnome that knows things others don't. Lol, don't fret, it happens to all of us one time or another out here in the pines, especially if you make a wrong turn and stumble across a pile of deer bones in the road and you misjudged the amount of time it would take to finish a hike and now the sun is setting faster than you would like it to. Usually, though, strange occurrences are just your mind playing tricks on you. The heavy breathing or a loud snort is probably from someone on horseback enjoying a trail ride in the forest nearby. And more than likely you'll run into a lifted 4x4 truck or dirt bike that signals to you that you're not that far from a parking lot and your car. But boy you'll have a story to tell friends later, won't you?"

This drawing of the Jersey Devil with its claws clutching a purple stemmed plant is a hint to its Piney name. *FINGERWEED* (Blue Vervain) and the Jersey Devil, along with other strange things, can be found in abandoned blueberry fields like the one we are hiking by now. Especially in wet meadows of the pinewoods.

Nearing the finish of our Piney gnome guided hike it's appropriate that we recognize the changing landscapes and how man has influenced the landscape for generations. Especially in the farming industry. The forests we hiked through, the trees, are as large as they have ever been. Before the area was made part of the National Pinelands Reserve, the trees were routinely harvested. And areas were cleared like this old, abandoned blueberry field for agriculture crops. We had heard about blueberry farming earlier in volume one. With so much going on in the Pine Barrens it makes you wonder why it was ever called barren land, doesn't it?

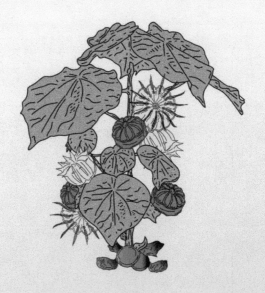

"Look to the edge of that row of blueberries," exclaimed Piney Joe. "People often mistake this plant for a surprise pumpkin plant growing in the backyard. But South Jersey farmers have first-hand knowledge of this pesky weed. Our Piney traditions call this ***CANDY PODS*** or, you who like Latin, Abutilon theophrasti. Grab one of those seed pods and watch hundreds of tiny seeds rush out onto the ground. Yeah, farmers don't like weeds that reseed themselves so easily as this one. And it loves to grow in the fields with our Silver Queen corn and the much-loved Jersey tomato."

That's number 19 of Pineycraft items that we've encountered on our hike. Did you know there are a few Pineycraft items in the Richardson Calendar, which totals 101 dried floral items, that were grown on many farms in South Jersey just like corn and tomatoes? Some farmers had plots set out for crops other than edibles, like wildflowers. Things like Baby's Breath, Dried Cockscomb, Purple Salvia, and Yellow Yarrow were also farmed. It's no wonder New Jersey is called the garden state. And if you drive through the Pine Barrens you'll see many U-pick farms, roadside fruit & vegetable stands, and hundreds of both large and small farms dotting the southern landscape. There is a bit of country in each of the 56 townships of the Pinelands.

Let's keep moving, won't be but a few moments longer before we reach the parking lot again and that concludes our tour of the pines with Piney Joe.

Now it's your turn to explore and find pictures by searching keywords:

- *"Eastern Black Snake"*
- *"Blue Vervain"*
- *"Abutilon theophrasti"*
- *"Verbascum blattaria"*

"Eww, or should I laugh out loud about the nickname or common name this plant was given way back when? This heres be the last lesson I'll impart on you today. Like two guideposts one on each side of the trail there." Piney Joe points to the plants' leaves, "You know we all do it. Let me whisper it to you: this plant is called **SCOUT'S TOILET PAPER** (also known as Common Mullein). The plant has big fluffy leaves that can be used in an emergency when you are in the woods and don't have any toilet paper. I know it's gross and funny at the same time, but it is true."

After this plant loses its pretty yellow flowers from the single green stalk, it goes into the seed stage. This is when it was harvested. It's a great thing. The plant stalk serves more than one purpose. Originally it is to produce seeds for the next generation to grow. But Pineys found another use for it. The plant is incredibly unique, and you would never mistake it for another plant. That unique look is why the stalk is harvested and placed in dried flower arrangements. The plant's shape is sturdy and enduring, so not only is it beautiful today but in ten years it will look the same as it does today.

In a thoughtful and admiring voice, Piney Joe says, "Plants used by us Piney folk introduces the thought of that the most famous Piney, Dr. Still. Have you ever heard of the 'Black Doctor of the Pines'? He who prescribed the use of locally collected medicinal plants just like this common Mullen which is still used today for many purposes like coughs in the form of tea and a tincture. Many know of Dr. Still for he helped comfort and cure many a good Piney family from what ailed em."

If you have been observant along this trek, you've probably noticed many strange things growing out of old trees or weird shrines out in the middle of nowhere that Piney Joe did not point out. Maybe he thought you wouldn't care to hear the story that went along with these oddities, or he was protecting the sites from any unnecessary disturbances. Sacred spaces—the smell of pine resin and the heat generated by the warming of the white sand roads and pine needles on a warm day is spiritual in nature. All these elements are repeated over and over a million times throughout the Pine Barrens giving the explorer unlimited sacred places to discover and enjoy on your own.

There it is, the parking lot and the ending of our adventure together!

Piney Joe is muttering under his breath, "It's hard to put into words. These sacred spaces are my home, and many other woodland animals and plants call them home. Humans are only guests to these places and as such one should show respect and not litter and make too much commotion breaking the peace and tranquility of the Pines. You noticed we passed by places that looked to once have been inhabited by someone. Indeed, I don't like to linger in places in the Pines where families once stood breathing in the pine air and making merriment, for now the places are full of ghosts. Maybe the ghosts are just my visions of those who came before us, and it scares me to think I'll be a ghost in this forest one day too."

In a more confident tone, "Peaceful patterns are transforming our forested areas across these great lands; green to red leaves being but one. More subtle in our Pine Barrens, but if you look, you can see them as we have seen them today. Being able to experience it firsthand is a mind-blowing experience. More and more people flock or escape to experience the solitude and safety of the open-air our forests provide for free. And you are free to move about in the woods like you couldn't in a shopping mall today. But we Pineys only ask that you not forget the stories I've shared and the memory of the Piney culture that you've experienced for yourselves. The simple act of reaching down and touching the seed head of a Foxtail or the soft top of a Cat's Paw connects you to the past. You can find the essence of the Richardson Calendar throughout the lands. See them and share them with friends and family. For knowledge is a treasure even us gnomes refuse to keep to ourselves. And it's freely given to those that respect our land and respect themselves.

PLANT LIST OF PINEY JOE'S ADVENTURE
(in sequential order)

*Native and non-native plants were harvested as part of the Richardson Calendar

11.   *CAT'S PAW* aka Eriophorum virginicum
12.   *PINEBALLS* aka Pinus rigida
13.   *QUEEN ANNE'S LACE* aka Daucus carota
14.   *PEPPERGRASS* aka Lepidium virginicum
15.   *PENNYCREST* aka Thlaspi arvense
16.   *MINIATURE WILD OATS* aka Glyceria obtusa
17.   *SNAKEWEED* aka Verbascum blattaria
18.   *FINGERWEED* aka Verbena hastata
19.   *CANDY PODS* aka Abutilon theophrasti
20.   *SCOUT'S TOILET PAPER* aka Verbascum thapsus

Thank you for coming along on this Piney adventure. We've been able to read about 20 different plants of the Richardson Calendar that are commonly found in the New Jersey Pine Barrens. Some of you may have been introduced to new concepts like the difference between a native plant or an invasive plant and how there is no such thing as a bad plant. Or how so many plants got common names, but their proper scientific names are most important. You also got to glimpse into the past of the people who lived in South Jersey and were called Pineys. How they lived and how they knew a bit about *woods magic* that helped them farm the woods, providing people with beautiful, dried flowers to decorate their homes. And this type of Piney, the Woods Piney, is one of ten types that still exist today. Along the journey, we hope you learned that learning is fun. And being able to recognize a plant growing outside by name just like you do friends and classmates is kind of cool. It's important to remember our friend's names along with the names of our friends growing alongside the road or out in a field.

The End

Piney Joe's Self-Guided Exploration Trail Map

But wait the adventure isn't over! Using the following illustrated trail map, you can jump in your car and go explore popular places in South Jersey and the New Jersey Pine Barrens and maybe get to see some of the 20 plants we learned about along the way. Hopefully, you discover a bit of the Piney woods magic and find a new favorite park to visit with family and friends. Good luck and safe travels Piney Explorers!

Trail Map Instructions. We would love you to share your adventures on social media by using the hashtag #pineyjoeadventures on any photos of your adventures to one of the 31 waypoints. There is a convenient checkbox for you to tick off as you go exploring. Remember before you go: an ounce of preparation is worth a pound of luck. A quick google or a phone call to one of the state-run parks may provide information that will change your plans. We highly recommend Mike McCormick's website as a great starting place to plan visits: Southjerseytrails.org.

Also on pages 141–142 we have grouped the destinations by county which might prove useful to you when planning your next exploration.

1. **Brendan T. Byrne State Forest.** Visit the state park office and grab a map or a souvenir. There is a pink blazed 52.7-mile hiking trail that traverses through the Pine Barrens that starts at Ong's Hat in Byrne State Forest and ends in Bass River State Forest. The Batona trail runs throughout the park and this featured fire tower is close to the highway on route 72. As you climb the stairs note the Eastern white pine trees that surround the tower and how high they are compared to the fire tower which is used by the forest fire service to protect against forest fires. There are several towers spread throughout the Pine Barrens and each is used to spot wildfires way out in the forest which can aid in prevention of dangerous large-scale wildfires.

☐

2. **Barnegat Lighthouse State Park.** Wonderfully preserved public spot in Long Beach Island, NJ, where you can walk along the jetty and or climb to the top of old Barney (the lighthouse). The views from the top overlooking the ocean are worth the harrowing trek up a gazillion stairs.

3. **Carranza Memorial.** A somber but neat piece of history tucked away in Wharton State Forest on Carranza Road, Tabernacle, New Jersey. Also, note the Batona Trail runs nearby which affords a short out and back trip on the trail from the Carranza Memorial parking area. After exploring or before you get to the memorial, checkout Nixon's General Store. It's an old local meeting place and great place to get a hoagie and a cold drink.

☐

4. Downtown Chatsworth and King of the Pines Buzby's Eatery & General Store. There are few better places to grab a bite to eat in the Chatsworth area than these two locals' favorites: Buzby's General Store built in 1865, a registered National Historical Site (Willis Jefferson Buzby est. 1891) & Hot Diggity Dog (est. 1989). Situated in between the two opposite sides of these Main Street businesses is a public dirt parking lot. It's an honored tradition among many Pine Barren's families to make a trip out to enjoy a hotdog and root beer on a summer's day at one or both of these fine establishments. While you are on the hot dog stand's side of the street walk a few paces to the sign featured here of the Central New Jersey Railroad of New Jersey's luxury passenger train called the Blue Comet. For a bonus on this trip keep traveling south from Main Street which turns to route 563 and in the Fall season you can see Ocean Spray's cranberry bogs bubbling with the little red rubies.

5. Double Trouble State Park. Located at 581 Pinewald Keswick Road, Bayville, New Jersey 08721. It has everything you could want in a Piney village. Once a historic cranberry operation along Cedar Creek, it takes just a little bit of imagination to see the ghosts of the one-time thriving village of Double Trouble. Miles of walking trails for all age levels.

☐

6. Franklin Parker Preserve. This Wobbly Hobbit Bridge can be located at Mile Marker 38 along the Batona Trail in the Franklin Parker Preserve in Chatsworth, New Jersey. Go to the New Jersey Conservation Foundation for more information on the trails and preserve. Note you can add this to your trip at the same time as planning to stop in downtown Chatsworth and Hot Diggity Dogs.

☐

7. Estelle Manor Park. Part of the Atlantic County Park System, these ruins and the boardwalk that twists through an Atlantic white cedar swamp are truly a sight to see. The boardwalk is the closest and cleanest way to experience walking among towering Atlantic White cedar groves that open to view the west bank of the Great Egg Harbor River in places. Stroller friendly.

☐

8. Lake Lenape Park East. Another diamond in the rough of the Pines, part of the Atlantic County Park System. Lake Lenape hosts a lighthouse that was never truly an operational navigation waystation. It had various uses over time: one being a place for children to camp in. Looking at a map it's sandwiched between Estell Manor Park to the south and Weymouth Furnace to the north. Today it is as photogenic as the day it was built in 1939.

☐

9. Lucy the Elephant. While Lucy is not located in the Pine Barrens, this is a "must view in-person" location just a stone's throw from the Pines. The look of amazement on children of all ages can be seen when onlookers first see Lucy in Margate City, New Jersey 08402. Restrooms and a great souvenir shop onsite. Couple a trip here with a trip to the nearby Absecon Lighthouse, and you've got a day of unforgettable memories. Warning. A restoration project began September of 2021 and is expected to last until Memorial Day 2022 closing Lucy to the public.

☐

Piney Joe

10. **Mullica River Trail.** As Piney as you can get, this walking trail runs from Atsion Recreation Area to Batsto Village in Hammonton, New Jersey for a total of 9.5 miles. Being these are both areas located in Wharton State Forest, see the state website for up-to-date details on camping and other fun offerings. Note when hiking in the Pine Barrens be prepared for bugs, wood ticks, mosquitoes, and the like.

☐

11. **Pemberton Railroad Station & Rail Trail.** Located at the Pemberton Rail-Trail North Branch section at 7 Fort Dix Road, Pemberton, New Jersey 08068. Walk along one of many rail-trails in New Jersey. This specific trail features many species of wildflowers that would not be encountered in the nutrient-poor recesses of the New Jersey Pine Barrens. For example, Spring Beauty, Jack-in-the-Pulpit, and Trout Lily. Once the North Pemberton Railroad Station Museum was open to the public and maybe one day again.

☐

12. Island Beach State Park & Reeds Road Trail. Pay your beach fee (set fee per vehicle) at the entrance to the state park. Be on the lookout for the tiny sign on the right of the road saying, "Reeds Road Maritime Forest Trail." After getting on the trail remember to be as quiet as possible while walking along and look for other people with binoculars around their necks as this is a premier place to see migratory birds, spring and fall. Also, the island is known for foxes. On the other side of the road are many different beach accesses to enjoy. Even before you get to Island Beach, may we recommend a detour to check out the Cattus Island County Park stop (later in the trail map). This is before crossing the Thomas A. Mathis bridge and onward to Seaside and Island beach.

☐

13. Great Bay Boulevard Wildlife Management Area (WMA) is in Tuckerton New Jersey. Home of many of our native plants and birds that reside along the Jersey Shore. But the most sought-after and slow-moving of the critters is the Diamond Backed Terrapin turtles. One can drive down Great Bay Boulevard at the right time of the year and see mothers nesting and crossing the road so be careful not to hit one. Note there are no restrooms along this 5-mile-long road. But there are plenty of local places before you get to the boulevard to get a bite to eat and use restrooms. Locals call Great Bay boulevard "seven bridges road" as at one time there were plans to have seven bridges built but only six are now in place.

☐

14. Plumsted Township Little Free Library with Piney Joe. Little Free libraries are a network of free libraries built and maintained by volunteers across the world. Nearly every community has at least one Little Free Library while Plumsted Township in Ocean County has two. Crafted by our illustrator Shane Tomalinas' family and donated by the author to the community. See how many others you can find. Maybe there is one in your own neighborhood.

☐

15. Weymouth Forge/Furnace. Iron is an element, but it can be found in the sandstone of South Jersey and was an important resource during the Revolutionary War period. This tiny park is another great stop in the Atlantic County Park System. Bring your camera as this place has been photographed by many talented photographers and a selfie is a must!

☐

16. **Whitesbog Historic Village.** Check their hours ahead of time as this unique place in the Pine Barrens is run by volunteers so the General Store may not be open (restrooms are in the General Store only), but the surrounding dirt roads along the beautiful cranberry bogs are open most days. Ask about their new membership benefits which supports Whitesbog Preservation Trust, a nonprofit 501(c)3 which operates the village. This gem is mostly unknown by many situated within the Brendan T. Byrne State Forest. So, grab a snack and a souvenir at the General Store before heading out for a walk along one of the many trails. And you can also drive along the many cranberry bogs with a regular non-four-wheel drive vehicle. Dog friendly walking.

☐

17. **Atsion Recreation Area.** Atsion Lake is only one part of the Atsion Recreation Area. In the summer months when it is open, it offers a family-friendly place to take a dip safely as it usually has a lifeguard on duty. Atsion Recreation Area is part of the greater Wharton State Forest. With over a hundred thousand acres Wharton has a lot to offer the Pine Barrens explorer. You have both Atsion and Batsto Village contained within. There is swimming, canoeing, hiking trails, and playgrounds, with the history of the NJ Pine Barrens all around you.

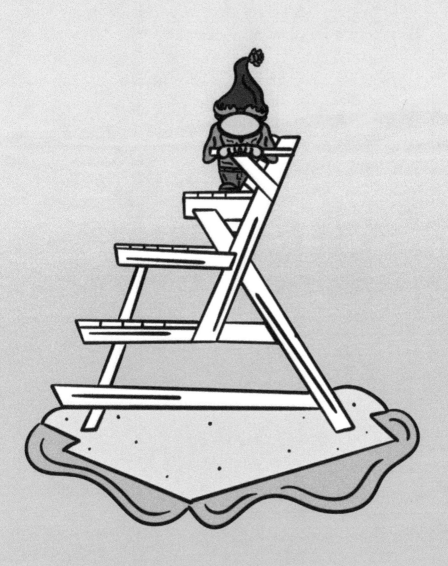

18. Batsto Village. This historic site is contained within the Wharton State Forest. Many of the original buildings, including the most photographed mansion in the Pine Barrens, are located on this state property. Our nation's history is comingled with this site as many a Revolutionary War cannonball was produced here. Today you can tour the site, visit the gift shop, hike, or canoe along the Batsto River. As with all state-operated parks, visit their website and or call ahead to confirm hours of operation and access details.

☐

19. **Cedar Bridge Tavern.** Another historic site like Batsto Mansion that has been preserved for future generations. The Revolutionary War or American Revolution also has a historical note here. Cedar Bridge Tavern is rumored to be the site of one of the last skirmishes of the revolution. It is in the town of Barnegat, part of Ocean County, and it would be great to add Painted Rock and a stop in Warren Grove to make it a full day of fun exploring down Route 539.

☐

20. **East Point Lighthouse.** Located along the Delaware Bay in Heislerville, New Jersey. It stands on the southern Bayshore where the Maurice River empties into the bay. This is a wonderful place to watch the breeding horseshoe crabs or to see many of our stopover shorebirds. Or a simple place to stop and dip your toes into Delaware. A nonprofit operates the East Point Lighthouse in an agreement with the NJ Department of Environmental Protection.

☐

21. Tuckerton Seaport Museum. This is more than four walls and a roof. The museum shows what it *was* and what it *is* to be a person of the New Jersey seashore. Find decoys of local ducks as well as the many vessels that were used in the local bay area to hunt and fish. Onsite situated along Tuckerton Creek is the Union Market & Gallery, which is a destination all its own; they serve up freshly brewed coffee, breakfast and lunch, and baked goods like no other.

☐

22. Edwin B. Forsythe NWR. The jewel of our National Wildlife Refuge system, "Brig" or "Brigantine," as many birders call it, is a place of refuge for migratory birds and a haven for many resident birds. Winter flocks of snow geese are a spectacle to witness in person. The eight-mile loop can be driven, walked, and or biked offering the adventurer many opportunities to view wildlife along the scenic shores. This site is federally managed so do view their website for hours of operation for both their gift shop and the "loop."

☐

23. Painted Rock of route 539 Lacey Township, NJ. Since 9/11 volunteers have maintained the site to represent our support for the military and as a reminder of all those who served. It is a very patriotic sight to see along the never-ending route 539 heading south to Warren Grove and Lucille's Diner.

☐

24. **Wetlands Institute of Stone Harbor, NJ.** With a quarter mile salt marsh trail on-site along with their educational facility, what's not to love? This site is outside the official Pine Barrens footprint. But with a walking trail and a top-notch education and conservation facility whose mission protects the wetlands, it's a must-visit of South Jersey.

☐

25. Greenwood WMA Webb's Mill Bog boardwalk. This is one of those places you have to visit in all four seasons as the boardwalk is poised over top of the flowing waters of Webb's Mill. And the fauna dramatically changes with each season. Several hundred feet contain a great introduction to the bogs of the Pine Barrens. If you are looking to see a carnivorous Pitcher Plant this is the place. The area can get wet, so muck boots are recommended. You could pair this with a trip to Cedar Bridge Tavern.

☐

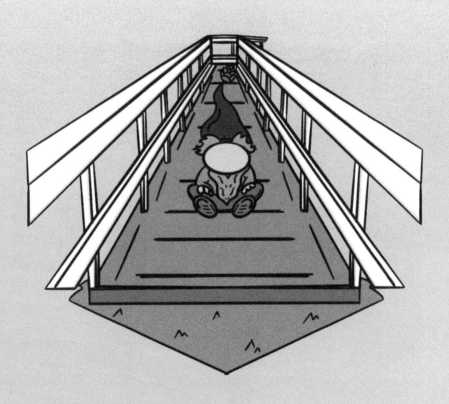

26. Woodford Cedar Run Wildlife Refuge. Their mission involves educating people of all ages with nature-based programming in addition to their Woodford Nature Center. And they take in injured animals for rehabilitation. This site is outside the official boundaries of the Pine Barrens but much of the habitat resembles the Pines. On your way to or coming back from Carranza Memorial, these two would be a good day outing combo. Note there are entrée fees and membership opportunities for this site.

□

27. Hereford Inlet Lighthouse. Admission is free to our third Lighthouse on the trail map. This one takes you to the furthest southern point just outside the Pine Barrens, for who doesn't love lighthouses? If you followed the trail map in sequential order you've already gone to these lighthouses: Barnegat Lighthouse, Lenape Lake Lighthouse (not a true lighthouse), Absecon Lighthouse (side trip from Lucy the Elephant), East Point Lighthouse, and Tucker's Beach Lighthouse Replica at Tuckerton Seaport Museum.

☐

28. Cattus Island County Park. Just off route 37 in Toms River, the park is situated along Silver Bay. There are seven miles of trails, and the Cooper Environmental Center has great nature-based exhibits open to the public. If you have toddlers and or a kid's heart, the playground is amazing too! Lots of different winged creatures are attracted to the unspoiled landscape and there is a butterfly garden at the center. Osprey viewing camera is indoors when available.

29. Popcorn Park Zoo. This animal sanctuary like no other is located in Forked River, Lacey Township. A nonprofit that requires an admission fee to the park where you can see zoo animals up close. It's way more than just your typical zoo though. Getting its name from popcorn treats that can be fed by visitors to the zoo animals. There is also a greater mission to take in injured animals and adopt out domestic animals like rabbits, cats, and dogs. Here is a Pine Barrens Zoo that captures your heart requiring you to come back again and again.

30. Warren Grove's Pygmy Pines. See the hilltop views for miles over the flat plains where Pygmy and or dwarf pine trees grow no taller than 5 or 6 feet. A word of caution the Pygmy pines are best viewed from the road. There are east and west plains off route 539 and route 72. Stop at Lucille's Diner in Warren Grove for some local advice and some of the best home cooking with pie.

☐

31. **Pinelands' farmstand named Charley's Place on Route 539 in New Egypt, NJ.** This is one of many Pinelands roadside stands that are a fixture to the region that was once said to be "barren," lending to the name Pine Barrens. But as you can see, there are dozens of farms in the 1.1 million National Reserve.

☐

Adventure with

Where To Explore Next

The seven counties (56 municipalities) that have parts of the 1.1 million acres of NJ Pine Barrens in them are Atlantic, Burlington, Camden, Cape May, Cumberland, Gloucester, and Ocean. Our Trail Map stops in five of those seven counties of New Jersey. Sites are listed below in alphabetical order. You can visit each location in any order you choose. This list helps to group them by county.

Atlantic
- Edwin B. Forsythe NWR #22
- Estelle Manor #07
- Lake Lenape Lighthouse #08
- Lucy the Elephant #09 (not in Pinelands)
- Weymouth Furnace #15

Burlington
- Atsion Recreation Area #17
- Batsto Village #18
- Brendan T. Byrne State Forest #01
- Carranza Memorial #03
- Downtown Chatsworth and Buzby's General Store #04
- Franklin Parker Preserve #06
- Mullica River Trail #10
- Pemberton Railroad Station & Rail Trail #11 (not in Pinelands)
- Whitesbog Historic Village #16
- Woodford Cedar Run Wildlife Refuge #26 (not in Pinelands)

Cape May
- Hereford Inlet Lighthouse #27 (not in Pinelands)
- Wetlands Institute of Stone Harbor #24 (not in Pinelands)

Cumberland
- East Point Lighthouse #20

Ocean
- Barnegat Lighthouse #02
- Cattus Island County Park #28 (not in Pinelands)
- Cedar Bridge Tavern #19
- Charley's Place on Route 539 in New Egypt #31
- Double Trouble State Park #05
- Great Bay Boulevard Wildlife Management Area (WMA) #13
- Greenwood WMA & Webb's Mill Bog boardwalk #25
- Island Beach State Park & Reeds Road Trail #12
- Lucille's Country Cooking Diner on Route 539 #30
- Painted Rock on Route 539 Lacey Township #23
- Plumsted Township Little Free Library with Piney Joe #14 (not in Pinelands)
- Popcorn Park Zoo #29
- Tuckerton Seaport Museum #21

Acknowledgments

Are the only people that read the acknowledgments section the people that are being recognized? I read the acknowledgments to see how thoughtful an author is. That being said, you the reader are usually never recognized for your contributions to the ongoing publication world. Without you, we wouldn't need to print so many wonderful books. For that, I say thank you! One such family, Mrs. Alessandra Montoya Rogers & fam, read the first manuscript and provided much-needed guidance to engage a younger audience.

The second huge acknowledgment is to my plant nerd friends: Mark Szutarski, Thomas Besselman, and the Illinois Botanizer Chris Benda—each professionals in their own right. Their knowledge of plants and willingness to share them has been most welcome in this endeavor. And I can't forget my herp friend Ryan Fitzgerald who ensured the accuracy in all things snake related. My editing team, including everyone at the South Jersey Culture & History Center, could not have been a more highly specialized and professional group to ever believe in such a project. The Center's leaders especially gave life to the book, Tom Kinsella and Paul W. Schopp. To my advanced readers or subject matter experts, your point of view and your most wanted opinions is what polishes the dirty piece of coal into a shiny diamond. Those readers are Alia Danch, Thomas Besselman, Justano Baratta, Josie Pullaro, Alyssa Tomalinas, and Hank Pear.

Lastly, none of my projects, this one included, could happen without the support of my family. To my wife and children, I say, "I love you the most even when you're honesty and much-needed criticism cuts the deepest." My wife, my muse and my best friend, thank you for your unwavering support. Who's had to hear me babble over and over as ideas and concepts took shape from our conversations. And lastly to my Sister Chrissy and Brother-in-law Eric who gave birth to Shane my famed illustrator (well they did other important stuff too). At a whim my sister volunteered Shane to bring an idea to vision which has led to the completion of a second book. The artwork inspired many a paragraph on these pages. And I am sure my nephew's artwork will also inspire you to get out and explore the New Jersey Pine Barrens. Yes, this book was a family affair, one that I hope has taught Shane that his art is an avenue worth pursuing. I say thank you. Oh, and before I forget, my niece Alyssa reviewed both manuscripts and provided valuable insight way above her 9 years of age (second draft age of 10). And finally, there aren't enough words to convey my appreciation for these three individuals. Through sheer luck or cosmic forces, after becoming friends with Anita Marie Lopez a writer who has followed in her mother Lillian Arnold Lopez's footsteps, we were able to bring to you part of a short poem Lillian penned entitled "Pine Gnome." Then there was Steven Carty who created Piney Joe's adventure backpack, and the almighty creator who molded and sewed Piney Joe into reality, Mrs.Linda Kelvy. Some names of support will surely be left off and for that we say sorry but for now we also want to thank the following for their assistance: Mike Kaliss the Pine Barrens Advocate, Hope Phillips our motto creator—Piney Tribe from the forest floor to the salty shore, Joe Makoviecki of Jackson Pines, and Lauren Vitagliano's beloved Pine Barrens Post a tiny house along the Mullica River in Sweetwater, NJ. Thank you. Thank you. Thank you.

Plant List of *Piney Joe's Adventure* (in sequential order):

1. Foxtail aka Setaria faberi
2. Elkshorn aka Lophiola aurea
3. Gumball aka Liquidambar styraciflua
4. Cattails aka Typha angustifolia
5. Rabbit's foot aka Lespedeza capitata
6. Star grass or Bell grass aka Oenothera biennis
7. Sweethuck or Sugarhuck aka Vaccinium pallidum
8. Banana cone aka Picea abies
9. Buttons aka Eriocaulon decangulare
10. Turkeybeard aka Xerophyllum asphodeloides
11. Cat's paw aka Eriophorum virginicum
12. Pineballs aka Pinus rigida
13. Queen Anne's Lace aka Daucus carota
14. Peppergrass aka Lepidium virginicum
15. Pennycrest aka Thlaspi arvense
16. Miniature Wild Oats aka Glyceria obtusa
17. Snakeweed aka Verbascum blattaria
18. Fingerweed aka Verbena hastata
19. Candy pods aka Abutilon theophrasti
20. Scout's Toilet paper aka Verbascum thapsus

Native and nonnative plants were harvested as part of the Richardson Calendar.

Plant Index. *Alphabetically sorted list includes Common Name, Piney Name, and Latin (botanical) Name:*

Abutilon theophrasti, 99
American Sweetgum tree, 21

Bananacone, 44

Blue Vervain, 96

Blunt Mana-grass, 87

Buttons, 47

Candy pods, 99

Cat's paw, 65

Cattail, 25

Common Mullein, 103

Daucus carota, 76

Eastern turkeybeard, 52

Elkshorn, 18

Eriocaulon decangulare, 47

Eriophorum virginicum, 65

Evening Primrose, 33

Field Pennycress, 84

Fingerweed, 96

Foxtail, 13

Giant foxtail, 13

Glyceria obtusa, 87

Goldencrest, 18

Gumball, 21

Lepidium virginicum, 80

Lespedeza capitata, 29

Liquidambar styraciflua, 21

Lophiola aurea, 18

Lowbush blueberry, 40

Miniature Wild Oats, 87

Moth Mullein, 92

Norway spruce, 44

Oenothera biennis, 33

Pennycrest, 84

Peppergrass, 80

Picea abies, 44

Pineballs, 69

Pinus rigida, 69

Pitch Pine tree, 69

Poor Man's Pepper, 80

Queen Anne's Lace, 76

Rabbit's foot, 29

Round-headed bush-clover, 29

Scout's Toilet paper, 103

Setaria faberi, 13

Snakeweed, 92

Star grass or Bell grass, 33

Sweethuck or Sugarhuck, 40

Tawny Cottongrass, 65

Ten-Angled Pipewort, 47

Thlaspi arvense, 84

Turkeybeard, 52

Typha angustifolia, 25

Vaccinium pallidum, 40

Velvetleaf seed pods, 99

Verbascum blattaria, 92

Verbascum thapsus, 103

Verbena hastata, 96

Xerophyllum asphodeloides, 52

About the Author

As a lifelong resident of New Jersey, William J. Lewis loves the diversity of the people of New Jersey and the landscapes of New Jersey's great outdoors. In the morning, one can have a lox and bagel sandwich for breakfast at a local deli in Allentown, New Jersey, and by lunch enjoy a WAWA hoagie at Island Beach State Park. All of which are things William enjoys doing. He deeply believes in environmental stewardship, seeks to serve others, and has served on various governmental and environmental nonprofits.

The most memorable moments so far in life, excluding family-related events, is a trip to the horn of Africa while working for the federal government and watching birds over a barbed-wire fence. If Mr. Lewis was asked, "What's the best advice you can give someone?" his immediate response would be, "Seek to serve." Serve others and the environment you are in. Through volunteer service, we find value in all things and experience life through others' eyes. These experiences have led him to become a writer, hoping to share his passions with the world. His debut book *New Jersey's Lost Piney Culture* hit the #1 Amazon Hot New Releases in January of 2021.

About the Illustrator

Shane Tomalinas is a New Jersey-based freelance artist and the lead merchandise designer for Piney Tribe. His love for drawing began at an early age, quickly turning into his passion in high school, where he had the opportunity to work with William Lewis on creating the character known as Piney Joe. Since the start of his work in Piney Tribe, Shane's art has stretched across social media, going viral on Tik Tok with his Matthew Lillard inspired fanart, getting his tiki design featured as the main attraction in Rocketsnail's newest video game *Boxcritters*, and having his fanart reshared by celebrities including David Dastmalchian . . . but he's only getting started! His works include a mix of variety including horror, fanart, archaeology, crypto-zoology, photography, and typography in both digital and physical displays.

He plans to pursue art in college, taking an apprenticeship in Graphic Design, and holding art fundraisers for his high school. There are even hopes to one day publish his adult horror novel, or more. Please check out Shane's website to purchase your original designs on t-shirts, masks, pillows, and even more at sjtbriker.redbubble.com. Check out his Instagram page for art reveals as well as fun projects he's invested in at Sjtbriker.

Gucci Green Afterword

You hear people call the Pines pristine. If you Google the definition the Oxford result states, "in its original condition; unspoiled or clean and fresh as if new; spotless." We've heard people use this all the time to describe the Pine Barrens, but the Pine Barrens haven't been pristine in well over 300 years. We had lumbering for the Atlantic white cedar, Chamaecyparis thyoides, in house construction, and it was used in the boat and ship building industry as well. The Pinus species was used for charcoaling to heat homes and also used to fuel the Iron industry. The Iron industry strip-mined the Pine Barrens from the late 1700s through the early 1800s. So the entire million acres of the Pinelands Reserve today in its current state has been cut over three times entirely by some estimates.

Today the Pine Barrens is a postindustrial forest. Alongside these manufacturing industries there is also agriculture production in the forms of arable crop farming, fruit trees and traditional Piney crops of blueberries and cranberries, and raising of cattle in the Batsto area. The glass making industry was prevalent in the Pines and so were paper mills. With all the industrial and agriculture production work the landscape was much different than what you see today. The forest today is probably fuller and more mature than it has been in over 300–350 years. And that's due to the resilience of the Pine Barrens which because of its low nutrients and pH values of the soil prohibits many invasive species from becoming established. This in turn helps to maintain the integrity of the Pine Barrens ecosystem.

That's not to say that there aren't any invasive species in the Pine Barrens. There are instances where invasives are becoming a problem but it is mostly due to the manipulation of the soil and the outside influx of nutrients from farming and or housing developments that allow the alien nutrients to drain into the Pine Barrens water table. Source pollution has occurred in both the Mullica and Batsto rivers which could have a far-reaching negative impact. These nutrients infiltrate the waterways of the Pine Barrens, negatively impacting our native flora which is probably our biggest threat to maintaining the balance in our unique ecosystem. Another negative to the Pine Barrens is the maintenance of the highways, both local and state, that introduce foreign roadside soils to maintain the public transportation road-ways by providing additional stabilization and nutrient-rich soil to grow nonnative grasses. These nonnative soils and grasses that were used for soil stabilization cause problems within the ecosystem. Also, some of the mowing practices along highways in the Pines in the past were disruptive to the flora, but we have recently seen improvements to the management of the public lands. These issues are identified by environmental-minded individuals that raise awareness to local and state authorities in hopes of maintaining the integrity of the Pinelands.

Another pressure is the suppression of forest fires. Forest fires can lead to a risk of human life and property loss. We continue to have development within the boundaries of the Pine Barrens in the forms of housing and commercial enterprise development. More and more encroachment into undeveloped areas of the Pines with the lack of forest fires has a larger cumulative negative impact on the overall ecology of the Pine Barrens. This system is highly dependent on fire. Forest fire is a needed disturbance. These natural disturbances help to increase early successional species which in turn increases the overall biodiversity of the Pine Barrens.

The Piney lifestyle could be described as a disturbance as well in the Pines. When Pineys went out, or more specifically the Woods Piney, and cut plant material or Pineycraft items that were in the Richardson Calendar, it was similar to a forest fire. The collection of plant material by these individuals for their subsistence living had a limited impact in the area which can be viewed as a positive disturbance. For example, when birch stems are cut by the Piney the plant may rejuvenate with increased new growth which can improve habitat for our native fauna. A good amount of the harvesting of Piney craft items or herbaceous vegetation was done after the mature plants went to seed-dispersing next year's growth which had no negative impact and possibly a positive impact on the species. The Pineys of yesterday who were dependent on this environment for their livelihood knew better than to over harvest as they had a financial interest in helping maintain the health of the forest. In today's world, unregulated harvesting could become a detriment to the environment and non-sustainable.

As amateur botanists, we want to debunk the stereotype of Pineys being a backwoods people with limited knowledge. They were very knowledgeable of local flora and practiced sustainable harvesting. Imagine trying to make a life like that of yesterday's Piney without today's technology? Could we even find the road that the Piney was living on today without GPS technology? Never before has a group of people been so misunderstood and so cruelly characterized as uneducated, untrustworthy, and dangerous by outsiders who did not understand their way of life. This has led to much doubt of Piney self-worth and to the value of their contributions to the culture of South Jersey and the greater historical tapestry of New Jersey. They were able to figure out how to live primitively in the woods. When society moved on, they had to adapt to living in the city but they still carried with them some of their old traditions and the tacit knowledge of our beloved Pine Barrens. Pineys of today have learned to adapt to a new world.

If you are part of today's Piney Tribe you know things others don't. Maybe the Sopranos show wasn't filmed in the Pine Barrens, but your imagination can point to many a road that could have been used by the mob hitmen. Roads to nowhere offer glimpses of ghosts of people from towns time forgot and nature swallowed whole. Do you have that kid (no offense as we hope to be a kid at 90) that's a cross between Smokey the Bear and Bill Nye the Science Guy? Or maybe an urbanite who loves to explore new places? In the back of the book along with a plant index is a trail map. Fully illustrated with key features to checkout in and around the NJ Pines. Travel along with Piney Joe as he fights geographic stereotypes and educates those who wish to preserve the environment and the melding of modern history with natural history and serves as a guide to the

1.1 million acres of the most unique place in the world (UNESCO named in 1983 a U.S. Biosphere Reserve). We hope you respectfully explore our Pine Barrens and listen to the lessons of Piney Joe. Oh, and as botanists, we encourage you to use the internet to look up each plant by its scientific name or Latin name. There are dozens of wonderful websites that give lots of information on how to distinguish one plant from another and some cool facts for each plant.

Sincerely,

Mark Szutarski & Thomas Besselman

The Other End